TO:

_____

FROM :

_____

DATE:

_____

PLAIN AND SIMPLE

JOURNAL

Created by Sue Bender
Illustrations by Sue and Richard Bender

Photographs courtesy of
Linda Reuther/Hearts and Hands

HarperSanFrancisco
A Division of HarperCollins*Publishers*

We are grateful to Linda Reuther/Hearts and Hands at Creekside Antiques, San Anselmo, California, for supplying us with the photographs of Amish quilts that appear in this work. All photographs are by Sharon Risedorph and Lynn Kellner.

All selections from *Plain and Simple* copyright © 1989 by Sue Bender.

Jacket and book design by Gordon Chun Design

FIRST EDITION

ISBN 0-06-250129-1

92 93 94 95 HCP-HK 10 9 8 7 6 5 4 3

This edition is printed on acid-free paper that meets the American National Standards Institute Z39.48 Standard.

I didn't know, when I first looked at an Amish quilt and felt my heart pounding, that my soul was starving, that an inner voice was trying to make sense of my life. *Finding a pattern for my own life.* That's what *Plain and Simple* was about.

My growing interest in the Amish took me by surprise. I went to live with the Amish to learn more about their quilts, but the quilts were only guides, leading me to what I really needed to learn, to answer a question I hadn't formed yet:

Is there another way to lead a good life?

Venturing into a seemingly timeless world, a landscape of immense inner quiet, I spent five summers living and working with Amish families. No one rushed. Each task was done with care. There was no hurrying to get to the "important things." For the Amish, it was all important. Five minutes in the early morning and five minutes in the evening were devoted to prayer. They spent the rest of the day living their beliefs. Their life was all one piece. It was all sacred—and all ordinary.

In contrast, my life was like a crazy quilt—a pattern I hated. Too busy, never having enough time, tempted in all directions, I wanted it all and never had the time to do all the things I said I wanted to do.

One day, while churning butter, I suddenly realized I had no more questions to ask. If there were answers, they were inside me. I went home and began to write. Actually, what I did was scribble. Jotting down details—remembrances, impressions, feelings—I let them pour out, unedited, uncensored.

After a while these scraps formed themselves into "patches." I collected them as I would the pieces for a patchwork quilt, not knowing what pattern would emerge.

My journal began with fragments. A fragmented life: bits and pieces of my history, Amish history, bits and pieces adding up, not adding up. Later, I realized I was making a quilt of my life—something that would tell my children who I am and what I came to value.

I have written one book, *Plain and Simple*. It took me five years to write 151 pages. During that time I came to believe in the value of keeping a journal—of doing the work—for its own sake. If the *Plain and Simple Journal* has a message, it is this: honor the search even if it is not what you expected or what you thought you wanted. It takes a lot of courage to get to know who you are and what you want.

- Write and write. *Don't judge.* Write it all down. Cut. Paste. Make a mess. Be ready for surprises.

- Write when you feel like writing, and write when you don't know what you want to write. Not knowing—and being comfortable with not knowing—that feeling of being led is a great discovery.

- Leave room for the unexpected.

- Move the patches around. Let your patches speak to you. Let them speak for you. This journal is your friend. Ask for help. Be ready for guidance.

- Remember: not risking can also be a risk.

- Ask yourself: "What really matters?" Keep that question alive.

- And, most of all, honor what you are doing. This is your quilt. There is no right way for it to be. Let these pages be filled with all the richness, complexity, contradictions, imperfections, and paradox that are uniquely you.

Perhaps each of us has a starved place, and each of us knows deep down what we need to fill that place. Maybe you have a dream incubating, not fully formed. Use this journal to test your dream. The very act of naming, appreciating, and accepting the patches in your life will illuminate your search.

To find the courage to trust and honor the search, to follow the voice that tells us what we need to do, even when it doesn't seem to make sense, is a worthy pursuit. I hope this journal will be about that search.

Sue Bender

We awoke Wednesday to overcast skies so we packed up & headed for Newport. The Breakers was magnificant, we tried lunch @ the mooring - 'what a nightmare' - + onto the Wharf Pub - where we were turned - around to a pleasant dining experience. We then toured the Oldest Synagogue in the Nation Touro. The day was exhausting - we all napped till 7pm + awoke for Pizza @ Dom's Corners + Ice Cream of course. Back home @ T.V. Bob arrived to wake Matthew once again - he hung - too long fell after Letterman + kissed me - yuk. Thursday on the Beach - I was doing my best to ignore him

Sheri was mad - but I wasn't
interested - that am I walked
the Beach & visited Big Good Bob!!
Hong & talked them to meet Rob
& Larry & Sue-- hit the Beach
& hung w/ Sue by Jeff's chair
She was really sweet. Back down
@ 4pm to see Bob have a Beer
& make a Date for 930 @ Andrea's.

Fran

50
75
___
125
___
105
70
___
195
140
___
335
45
___
380 WP

Helen

5
115
___
120
75
___
195
-60
___
135
60
___
195
95
___
299
105

F
420
90
510

H.
395
395

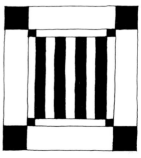

Susan Stephenson
401. 377. 4712
- Back on Monday 9.pm.
- so headed back down the beach. lost
Jeffrey's Ray Bans. (no that was Friday's walk)
Well we went to dinner @ Cody's - a
bit of a nightmare - as usual. I also
had to turn Bad Bob down for dinner +
the 🐒 factory. So we get in @ 830a
I'm getting ready to meet Bob.
+ you know who comes a knockin'
+ waking up Matthew. He hung + like
an idiot - I extended the invite for him
to come out - HELP!! - Thank god Big Bob
was understanding. It was like a
scene from a movie- meeting Bob
behind the fica tree - sitting between
the 2 Bobs at the bar. I felt very
bad + uncomfortable -
Bob. 1 gave me a pin
+ was very nice although
I just was not attracted
to him

Listening to your heart, finding out who you are, is not simple.

■

It takes time
for the chatter to
quiet down.
In the silence of
"not doing" we
begin to know what
we feel.

Can an object

go straight to

your heart?

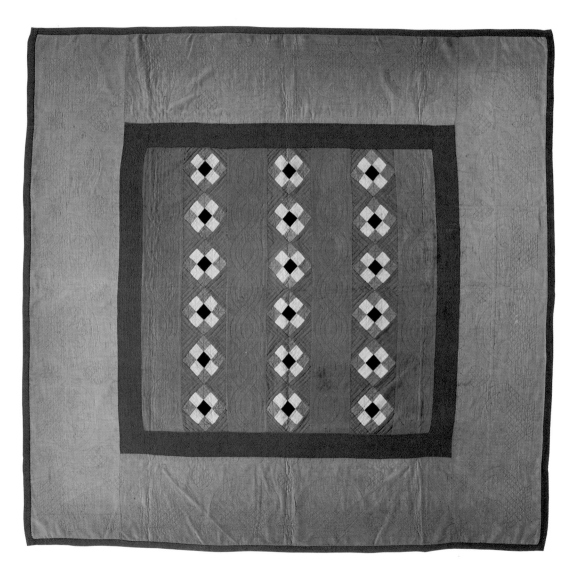

■

If we can listen
and hear what is
being offered, then
anything in life can
be our guide.

Lists engulf us—
creating the
illusion that our
lives are full.

■
■■
■

The quilts seem
silent, a "silence
like thunder."

■
■ ■

Sometimes we
confuse what we do
with who we are.

■

Lots of things we

don't get to choose.

It takes a lot of
courage to know
who you are and
what you want.

Diamond in the Square,
ca. 1930, Amish,
Lancaster County,
Pennsylvania (Hearts
and Hands Antiques,
San Anselmo, California)

Making a choice—
declaring what is
essential—gives
meaning to the things
that remain.

To simplify we have
to say no.

Each time I looked
at the quilts, my
busyness stopped.
The fragments of
my life became still.

Variable Star, ca. 1920,
Amish, Ohio (Hearts and
Hands Antiques, San
Anselmo, California)

There is a spirit
guiding us, in ways
we often don't
understand and
don't need to
understand.

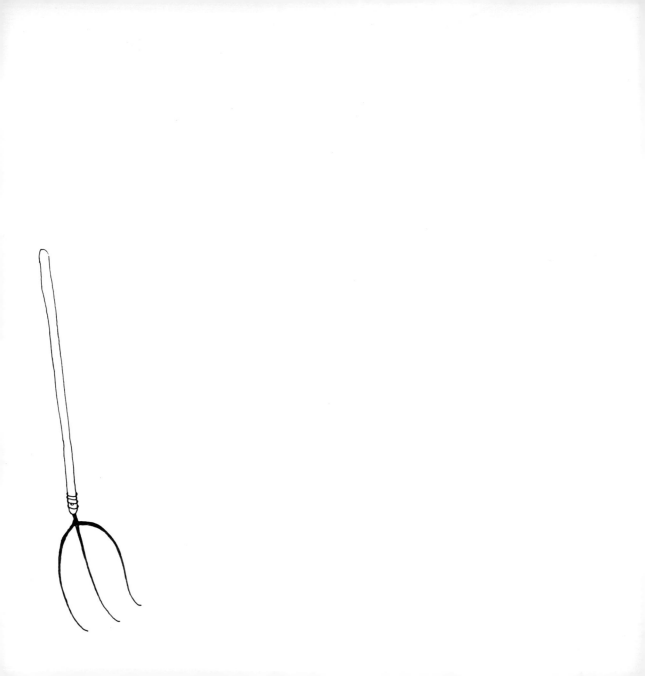

■ ■
■ ■

Any type of work
can be meaningful.
It's the spirit in
which you do it
that makes the
difference.

■

For the Amish, everything is a ritual. Doing the dishes, mowing the lawn, baking bread, quilting, canning, hanging out the laundry, picking fresh produce, weeding—no distinction is made between the sacred and the everyday.

Onepatch, ca. 1925,
Amish, Ohio (Hearts
and Hands Antiques,
San Anselmo, California)

An Amish woman told me, "Making a batch of vegetable soup, it's not right for the carrot to say I taste better than the peas, or the pea to say I taste better than the cabbage. It takes all the vegetables to make a good soup!"

A celebration of the

ordinary.

■■
■■

How can a quilt be
calm and intense at
the same time? Can
an object do that?

The Amish honor
the daily practices;
an object cared for
in a home can turn
into a shining thing.

For the Amish,
making a doll or a
quilt is no more
special than canning
green beans or
making a cake.

The Amish way is
full of connections.

Continuous Nine-patch,
Crib Quilt, ca. 1930,
Amish, Indiana (Hearts
and Hands Antiques,
San Anselmo, California)

Which of today's
tasks were a chore?
Which were fun?
For the Amish
there was no
separation.

Sunshine and Shadow,
ca. 1930, Amish,
Lancaster County,
Pennsylvania (Hearts
and Hands Antiques,
San Anselmo, California)

The ordinary can
be extraordinary.

The Amish live
what they believe.
Their life is their art.

■
Order calms.

Our attitude
toward the world
resonates in the
objects around us.
They reveal our
intention.

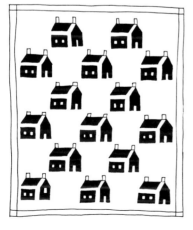

Our homes reflect
who we are and what
we value.

There is a big
difference between
having many choices
and making a choice.

Accumulating
choices is a way of
not having to make
a choice.

The world can
come to us in
fragments, but
the fragments
themselves are not
the enemy. If your
pattern is strong
enough, they will
form a whole.

Crazy Quilt, 1936, Amish,
Lancaster County,
Pennsylvania (Hearts
and Hands Antiques,
San Anselmo, California)

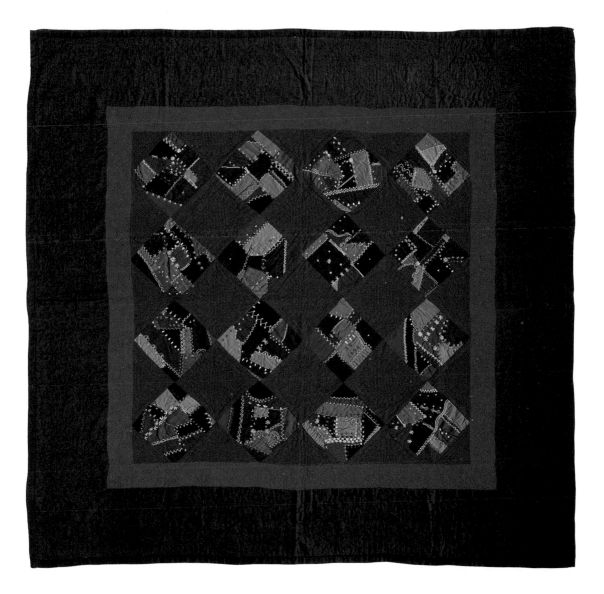

Simplify and then go deeper, making a commitment to what remains.

Finding a balance

we can live with . . .

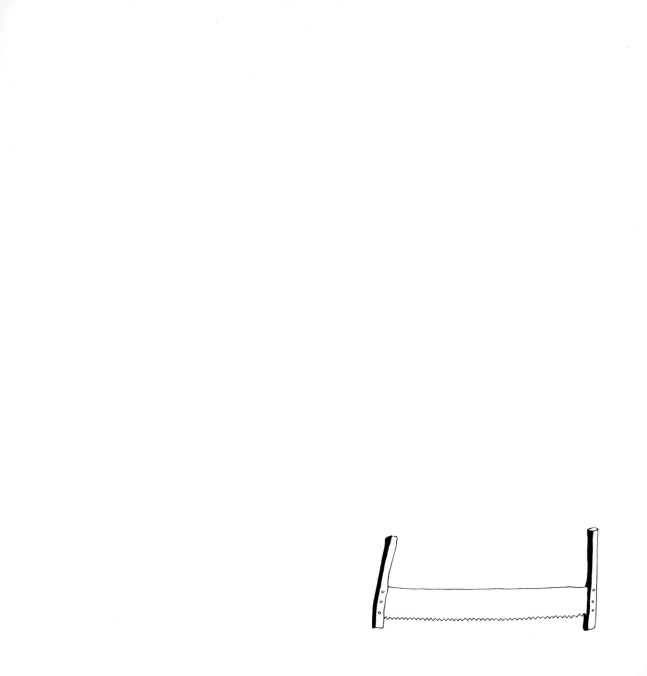

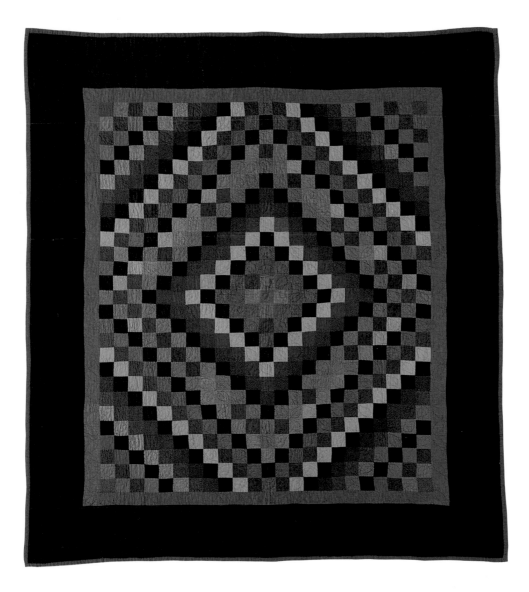

Satisfaction comes
from giving up
wishing we were
doing something
else—or being
somewhere else.

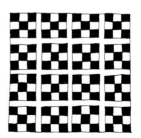

When you seek to
be special, only a
few things in life
will measure up.

Nothing you are
doing is wasted
time.

There are no
shortcuts.

Learning to trust,
no matter what life
turns out to be, is a
great discovery.

A living faith is one
that gets constantly
tested.

In that tiny space
between all the
givens is freedom.

■■
■■

Am I a successful
human being, not
only a success?

An impasse is
another marker on
the way.

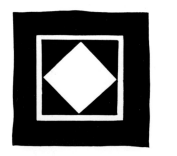

Basket Variation,
ca. 1920, Amish, Ohio
(Hearts and Hands
Antiques, San Anselmo,
California)

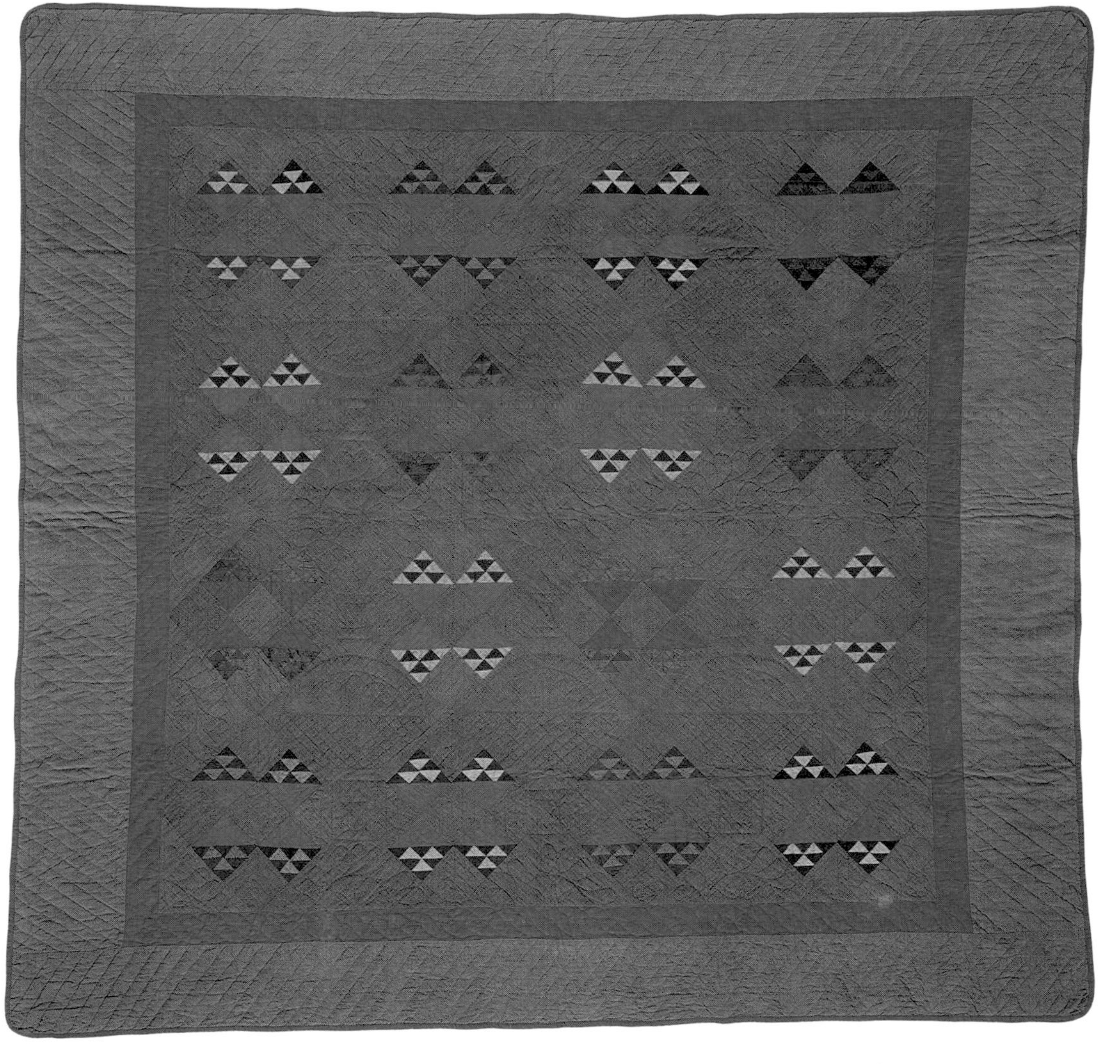

Satisfaction comes
from doing the work
over and over and
beginning to value a
high standard.

The need to be
special and stand
out, the need for
communality, to be
part of the whole,
the hunger to
belong, to be one
among the many—
these equally
competing,
conflicting values
are part of each
of us.

It's time to celebrate
the lives we do have.

■

Piecing together
the paradox—
making peace with
the paradox,
finding a balance
in some larger
sense, so that a life
can feel whole.

To reconcile our
seeming opposites,
to see them as
both, not one or
the other, is our
constant challenge.

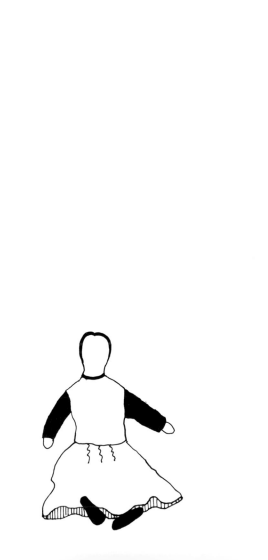

There is an old
me, a new me, an
imperfect me, and
the beginning of
a new acceptance
of all the me's.

■■
■■

Continue working
on your "quilt."
It will tell you
something about
the life you've lived
and the things
you've come to
value.

Trip Around the World,
ca. 1925, Amish,
Lancaster County,
Pennsylvania (Hearts
and Hands Antiques,
San Anselmo, California)

■■
■■

And we have

another choice—

to accept what

we didn't get

to choose.

■

Life's all about

moving your

patches around.

We don't need
reasons for doing
what we do.
Learning to follow
your heart is reason
enough.

Looking for
certainty and
finding comfort
in uncertainty.

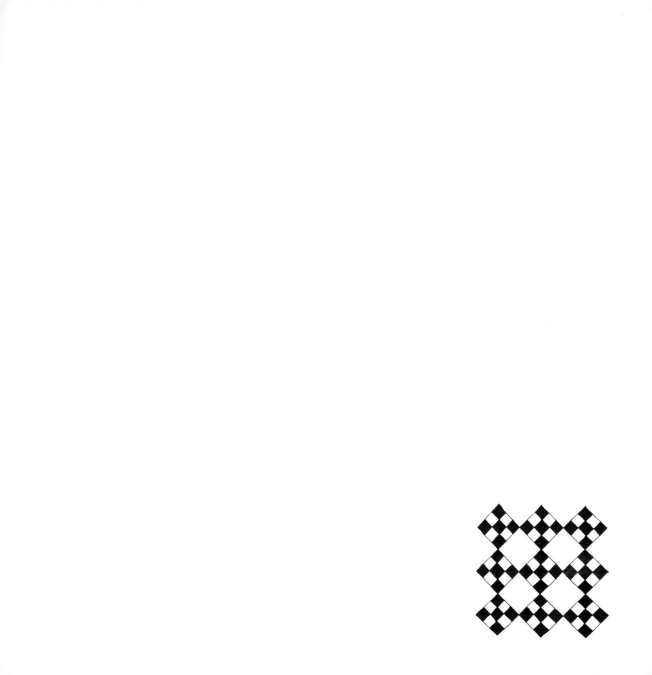

Leave room for the
unexpected.

The Amish often
leave a space in
their quilts—
a seeming mistake
in the midst of their
well-thought-out
plans—to serve as
an opening to let
the spirit come in.

Diamond in the Square,
ca. 1930, Amish,
Lancaster County,
Pennsylvania (Hearts
and Hands Antiques,
San Anselmo, California)

Miracles come after
a lot of hard work.